# Early Artisans

## Bobbie Kalman

**The Early Settler Life Series**

Toronto
New York

# Crabtree Publishing Company

*To my aunts, uncles, and cousins*

*A special thanks to the following people without whose help this book would not have been possible:*

**Senior editor:** *Lise Gunby*
**Researcher and editor:** *Susan Hughes*
**Assistant editors:** *Maria Protz*
*Mary Ann Horgan*
**Freelance editor:** *Dan Liebman*
**Design and mechanicals:** *Diane Taylor*
*Nancy Cook*
**Photographers:** *Sarah Peters*
*Peter Crabtree*
*Maria Protz*
*Lise Gunby*
*Diane Taylor*
**Picture researcher:** *Noel Rutland*

Copyright © 1983, 1989, 1992 Crabtree Publishing Company

*Cataloging in Publication Data*

*Kalman, Bobbie, 1947 -*
*Early Artisans*

*(Early settler life series)*
*Includes index.*
*ISBN  0-86505-023-6 hardcover*
*ISBN  0-86505-022-8 softcover*

*1. Handicraft - History - 18th century.*
*2. Handicraft - History - 19th century.*
*3. Cottage industries - History - 18th century.*
*4. Cottage industries - History - 19th century.*
*I. Title.    II. Series.*

*TT18.K34 1983      745.5'09'03      LC 93-30697*

350 Fifth Ave, Suite 3308
New York, NY 10118

R.R. #4
360 York Road
Niagara-on-the-Lake, ON
Canada  L0S 1J0

73 Lime Walk
Headington, Oxford 0X3 7AD
United Kingdom

# Contents

# The essential artisans

When we talk about crafts today, we think of hobbies. The crafts of the early artisans were not hobbies. They were jobs. Artisans had special skills. They used them to earn a living. When an artisan's skill was needed in the community, he or she lived and worked there. When the demand for an artisan's skill was limited, the artisan often moved to another village or traveled from place to place. Some artisans were farmers.

The early artisans were a necessary part of the settler community. They made the articles that the settlers needed. The settlers could buy beautiful furniture for their homes. They could buy pots and jugs, barrels and tubs. They could have their horses shod by the blacksmith. They could have comfortable shoes made.

Artisans helped to attract new settlers to a village. They provided goods that made the lives of the settlers more comfortable. The artisans' shops were places for people to meet. When the weather was bad, the farmers often gathered their broken tools and headed over to the blacksmith's shop. Their friends would also be there, getting tools repaired. Meeting at the shop was a good way to catch up on the village news. Sometimes one of the farmers brought along a fiddle. The settlers then got down to some serious singing and dancing!

*The blacksmith shop was important to the settler community. The blacksmith not only shod horses, he also made tools for the farmers,*

utensils for the kitchen, and parts for other artisans.  The blacksmith in this picture is putting tires on the wheels the wheelwright has made.  Artisans made the settlers' lives more comfortable.

# The crafts of living

*Before Joseph came to this country, he had never used an ax! He soon learned carpentry. He built a comfortable house from the trees on his land. He filled his home with wooden tables, chairs, dressers, and beds. He made wooden dishes and tools. Joseph can now make almost anything out of wood!*

*Round tree trunks were squared to make beams for buildings. One man sits at a planing vise. When he pushes the foot peddle forward, the vise grips the wooden peg he is planing. The man is planing the peg to a point. Pegs were used instead of nails in many buildings.*

*A barn-raising was enjoyed by the whole community. Everyone was a carpenter for the day! The frame was built on a stone foundation. How many trees do you think were used to build this frame? Many of the barns erected by the settler families are still standing today.*

*When the weather is not good enough for fishing, this fisherman whittles his time away. He has carved the base of a toy sailboat. The boys are eager to see if it will float.*

# Carvers and whittlers

I love the smell of wood and the feel of it under my fingertips. When I carve a piece of wood, I discover its beautiful texture and grain. I never know what my hands will whittle. There seems to be a magic in the wood which guides the shape. I begin to carve and after a few minutes I think, "Of course, this can only be a figure of a deer," or "This must be a small boat." I love to carve children's toys. Children can feel and see the beauty in a finely carved object. They love to play with a toy made of wood.

## Wood is beautiful

*Grandfather is making a flute for his grandson. Christmas is coming. Grandfather has also built a tiny wooden house for his granddaughter.*

I began carving many years ago. I am a trapper. I spend many weeks alone on the trap line. One day, I happened to find a beautiful piece of wood lying in the snow. That evening I began to explore it with my knife, cutting here, chipping there. Soon there were eyes peering out at me, and then a nose. The face of a raccoon was taking shape in my hands!

# Whittling time away

Many trappers, hunters, lumberjacks, and sailors carve in their spare time. Most of us are amateur whittlers. We carve toys for children, decoys for our duck hunting, and weather vanes for our houses. We whittle candlesticks and pretty little boxes. We make whistles and noisemakers. I know a few talented people who can carve fiddles. Listening to a wooden fiddle is like listening to the trees sing.

# Carving out a living

Some carvers are professionals. They carve to earn their bread. They usually begin as apprentices in cabinetmakers' shops. They learn to work with the lathe, shaping the legs of chairs with it. They learn to use the lovely grains in the wood as patterns across the cabinets, chairs, and tables.

Some woodcarvers become experts at carving figureheads. Have you ever seen a figurehead on a ship? It is a stirring sight. A figurehead is usually a magnificent human or animal shape. It sits at the prow of a ship and breathes the strong sea breezes. The figurehead keeps the ship safe on its voyages. Its beauty and pride protect the ship from enemies. The shipbuilder will ask only a very fine carver to make a figurehead.

Other woodcarvers make shop signs in the forms of animals, clocks, gloves, or boots. The shape of the sign tells a customer what the shop sells.

# The reward of laughter

I would not enjoy earning my living as a wood-carver. I admire the skill of the professionals, but for me, the joy of working with wood is payment enough. My reward is the delight in children's eyes. I see it when I give them toys carved especially for their pleasure.

*Cindy's toys are special because they were made by people she loves. Grandfather carved her big doll. Grandmother sewed her rag doll. Her older brother made Cindy a kaleidoscope. And Mother made Cindy a basket for all her toys! Homemade toys never seemed to break.*

*Many children did not go to school. They learned their skills from the artisans in the community. Andrew is an apprentice in the blacksmith shop. He is learning to be a blacksmith by working for the village blacksmith. Mr. Cook teaches Andrew to read when there is no work to be done.*

# Learning the crafts

There were many talented artisans. How did they learn their skills? The settlers were able to teach their children some basic skills, such as building, woodworking, and making clothes. However, in order to become artisans, children had to learn from the specialists themselves. Many artisans took children as **apprentices.** An apprentice was both a student and a worker.

## Hard work and long hours

In many European countries, there were laws that apprentices and artisans had to obey. Some communities in this country also had laws about hiring apprentices. Other places had no laws. Many apprentices were forced to work long hours.

## Choosing a trade

How did apprentices choose their trades? They usually did not. Parents chose careers for their children. Sometimes there were not many choices. Children were apprenticed to the artisans who were willing to teach them.

An apprentice usually lived in the house of the artisan. Some apprentices were treated as part of an artisan's family. They agreed to work and learn from artisans for a certain period of time, usually seven years. The artisan gave the apprentice shelter, food, and clothing, but no wages. Some artisans taught their apprentices to read, write, and do sums.

*Mr. Walsh owns a cobbler shop. He fixes shoes. When business is slow, Mr. Walsh travels from village to village. He goes to people's homes and offers to mend their shoes. He was asked to repair an umbrella at this home.*

# Rules for apprentices

Apprentices worked from early morning until late at night. They ran errands, delivered the finished products, and collected payments. Apprentices also had to find time to learn the skills of their trades. Some apprentices agreed not to marry while they were in training. They promised to stay out of taverns. They vowed to keep the secrets of their trades. Some apprentices promised not to leave the house or shop without permission. Those who broke the rules were sometimes beaten. Apprentices had to work hard and long, but they would have valuable skills when they finished the years of training. A boy usually served an artisan until he was 21. Female apprentices served until they were between 16 and 18.

# Traveling workers

When apprentices finished their training, they became **journeymen**. Journeymen were fully trained but did not have their own shops. After working in the same shop for seven years, an apprentice looked forward to traveling. Journeymen often worked twelve hours a day, six days a week. They were paid high wages and their employers usually provided free room and board. When journeymen had saved enough money, they settled down to open their own shops. Sometimes artisans traveled with their tools. They were called **itinerants.** They lived with one family until they finished work for that family. Then they moved on and made or repaired items for another family.

# The skills of the cabinetmaker

As communities grew, cabinetmakers opened shops. Cabinetmakers were carpenters who made fine furniture. They were creative as well as skillful. The furniture made by the early cabinetmakers is still strong and beautiful. Many people collect these antiques. Cabinetmakers shaped the pieces of wood according to special designs. Sometimes they borrowed one another's patterns. This cabinetmaker shows his **inlays.** They are his own designs. By putting these inlays or designs into his furniture, the cabinetmaker created unique pieces of furniture.

The early cabinetmakers did not have machines. They used hand tools made of wood and metal, such as saws and chisels. They used **augers** to drill holes into wood. The workbench of the cabinetmaker was a thick wooden table. **Vises,** or clamps, were attached to the bench. Vises held the pieces of wood steady. The artisan, above, shapes a piece of wood with a **plane.** A **router** was used to cut grooves into the furniture. Cabinetmakers preferred to work with walnut, cherry, maple, and pine. These woods grew plentifully in the thick forests.

The **lathe** was a useful power tool for shaping wood. There were different kinds of lathes. Some were operated by hand, others by water. This artisan is using a lathe operated by foot. He cuts grooves into the wood as it turns. The piece of wood will be the leg of a table.

This table leg took many hours to finish. After pieces of furniture were made, they were put together. The parts were connected firmly at the **joints**. The joints had to meet perfectly. If they did not, the furniture would be crooked. Nails were not necessary to hold the joints.

The last step was to **finish** the wood! A finish is the surface coat put on wood. Wood was sanded until it was as smooth as skin. Then the cabinetmaker coated it with stains, dyes, shellacs, oils, varnishes, or beeswax. This protected the wood from scratches, cold, and heat.

The cabinetmaker shines the chair once more. His customer will pick it up soon. In the villages, customers often paid for furniture with lumber. Lumber was as good as money to the cabinetmaker. He could use it to make more furniture!

# Making music

The settlers loved music. When their work
was done, they took out their fiddles, guitars,
recorders, and flutes. Most of their musical
instruments were brought from Europe. Sometimes cabinetmakers made pianos, harpsichords,
and spinets. Musical-instrument makers
also opened up shops in this country. Often,
artisans who specialized in making instruments
were not able to earn a good living from
their craft because it took so long to make
one instrument. Sometimes they had to farm
or do other work on the side.

*Mother accompanies Hans as he practices his
violin piece. Peter and Gretel pay attention.
Their turn is next. The whole family plays at
night. Father conducts the orchestra!*

## Choosing wood that sings

Musical instruments were made from the
wood of carefully chosen trees. The best
trees were those grown in the poorest soils.
These trees grew stronger because of the
minerals contained in the earth. When hit
with an ax, the wood of these trees seemed
to "sing." Apprentices to musical-instrument
makers were taught how to find the trees
that sang. The blocks of wood that were
cut from these trees were aged a long time
before they were carved into instruments.

*Bess and Marnie spend hours playing music.
They are often asked to perform in public.*

*The artisan plays the lute that he has just made. The lute was a popular instrument, but in later days, the guitar became more common.*

*Grandfather tunes his violin as Kathryn looks on. She loves the sound of his violin. It was made with great care by the village artisan.*

## Fine tuning

The artisan used spruce for the soundboard or **belly** of the stringed instrument. Spruce was strong and had good tonal quality. The backs of the instruments were made of maple. The front of the **fingerboard** was carved from ebony. Violins, lutes, and guitars were never nailed. Their parts were glued together. When the instrument was completed, it was coated over and over with varnish. The varnishing process took months. Up to twenty coats of varnish were applied. Each coat was allowed to dry before the next coat was put on. After the final layer of varnish was dry, the violin or guitar was polished to a brilliant luster. It was ready to be strung and sold.

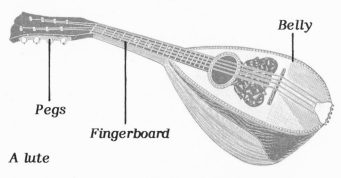

*Belly*

*Pegs*

*Fingerboard*

**A lute**

## Faster but not better

As factories were built, many instruments could be made at the same time. Instruments that were made in factories were cheaper than hand-made instruments. The factories, however, could not make musical instruments of the highest quality. Nothing could match the wonderful quality of musical instruments made by the hands of the early artisans.

*Elizabeth is spinning wool into threads. The spinning wheel stretches and twists the wool fibers so that they form strong yarn. Elizabeth turns the wheel by using a foot pedal. After the wool is spun, she can knit thick socks and sweaters.*

*Jane is the village weaver. Many settlers spun their own wool, but weaving on a loom was a complicated craft. Jane takes yarn and strings it on the frame of the loom. Jane guides the* **shuttle,** *which weaves the yarn into fabric. Fabric woven on a homemade loom was called* **homespun.**

*Alice has just finished making hand-dipped candles. She dipped the wicks into hot, liquid wax. The wax was called tallow. It was melted animal fat. After each dip, she let the tallow on the wicks cool. Each dip added another layer of wax. Candles were the settlers' only source of light at night.*

# The home arts

Almost everything used by the settlers had to be made from scratch. The settlers used products from plants and animals for making their clothes. Wool from sheep was spun into yarn for knitting and weaving. Fibers from the flax plant were woven into linen. Animal hides and furs supplied warm boots, coats, and mittens. Soap came from the ashes of burned wood. Mattresses were stuffed with fine goose feathers. Beautiful thick blankets were quilted from scraps of material.

The settlers skilled in these household arts were usually women. Women were the artisans of the home. In the early days, men usually worked at jobs outside the home. During a time when people had to work hard every day just to keep themselves clothed and fed, it was often simpler for men and women to have different tasks. Today, men and women work side by side at the same professions.

*Daniel is stitching deerskin to make moccasins. He is wearing a finished pair. The Indians taught the settlers how to make these comfortable shoes.*

The shoes that were made to order were the most comfortable. Shoemakers also made standard sizes of shoes. These shoes were made on **lasts**. Lasts were wooden or metal models of a human foot. In the early days, both the left and the right shoes were the same shape. This shoemaker checks a pair of shoes. Some of the shoes behind her were made on lasts. They will be sold at the general store.

# The shoemaker

The early settlers needed sturdy shoes and boots. They had to walk great distances. Shoes were expensive. Sometimes a husband and wife shared one pair of shoes. Some people went barefoot during the hot weather in order to keep their shoes from wearing out.

Some shoemakers traveled from house to house. A shoemaker stayed with one family until all the family members had shoes made or mended. It took one day for a shoemaker to make a pair of shoes. Sometimes, the shoemaker lived with a large family for several weeks!

Other shoemakers opened their own small shops. Shoemakers always had big windows in their shops because they needed good light for their work. When the neighbors dropped in for a chat, the shoemaker sat on a low bench, hunched over some work. On one end of the bench there was a circle of leather nailed over a hole. This was the shoemaker's seat. The other end of the bench was divided into sections for pegs and nails.

## Made to measure

Customers usually brought their own leather to the shoemaker. They placed their bare feet on the leather and the shoemaker traced the outlines. The sole or **tap** was cut from the heaviest hides of cattle or oxen. The top pieces of the shoe, called **uppers**, were made of soft leather, such as calfskin or goatskin. Tin or wooden patterns were laid on the leather, and the uppers were cut out.

Holes were worked into the leather with an **awl.** Then the tap was sewn to the uppers with a needle and thread. The thread was waxed with beeswax to make it strong and waterproof. The shoe could also be pegged together. Wooden pegs were driven into the holes to attach the pieces of the shoe together. The shoemaker preferred to use pegs because thread could stretch or break in damp weather.

Parents often bought their children shoes that were a little too large. The children wrapped their feet in woolen cloth to fill the extra space in their new shoes. Before many months passed, the shoes would fit perfectly.

*The shoemaker enjoys the fresh air as he sits on his bench near the window. He uses a special hammer which does not scrape the leather.*

*The shoemaker is getting some unexpected help. Have you ever heard the story of the shoemaker and the elves? Find the story in your library.*

*The settlers often made their own cloth. They could also buy cloth from the general store. Some settlers waited for peddlers to bring new materials from the large towns and cities. Grandmother wants to have a dress made from the beautiful linen. Grandfather may buy some linen for a shirt.*

*The dressmaker has just delivered Matthew's new suit. There is no tailor in the village, so the dressmaker also sews men's clothes. Matthew's sisters are curious to see if the seams are strong and the fit is right. Matthew is moving to the city to look for a job. He wants to look his best!*

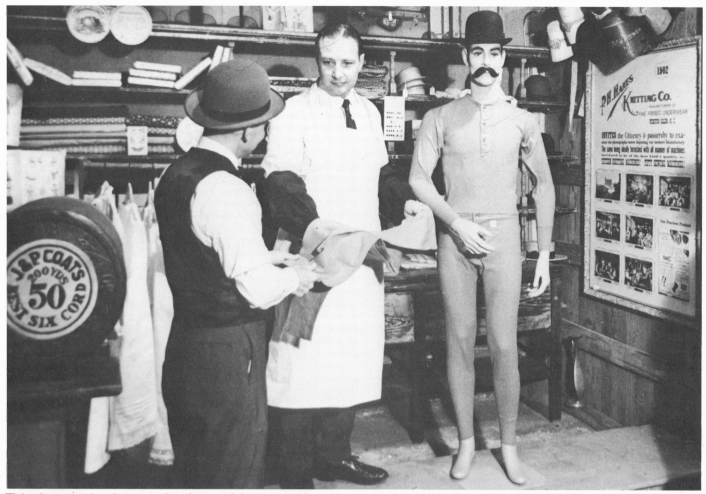

*This dummy is about to be dressed in a sample suit made by the tailor. The tailor's shop is in a corner of the general store. The storekeeper is interested in buying a new suit.*

# Clothes

Have you ever sewn something for yourself or for a friend? The early settlers not only made all of their own clothing, but they also made their own fabrics. They wove cloth and then made dresses, aprons, shirts, and britches.

There were always people in the community who had a special talent for designing and making clothes. Those who could afford to pay for their clothes had them made by these people. **Tailors** stitched clothes for men. **Seamstresses** sewed ladies' fashions.

## The tailor

As communities grew, tailors took on apprentices to help them finish their many jobs. Tailors taught their apprentices sewing techniques. They used different methods to make coats, cloaks, riding hoods, trousers, and shirts. The goal of every apprentice was to sew a garment as quickly and efficiently as possible.

## The seamstress

The seamstress, or dressmaker, was also a professional. She often had her own dress shop, but was willing to go to her customers' homes for measurements and fittings. She took the tools of her trade with her: pins, needles, thread, thimbles, scissors, beeswax, and tape measures. Customers usually took material to the dressmaker's shop. The dressmaker also kept a few rolls of fabric in stock. She made samples of the styles she was able to create. She dressed dolls in these fashions and placed them in her shop window. The dolls wore the latest styles and tempted women to enter the shop and order a new dress.

# Hatters

Hatters designed, made, and sold all sorts of hats. **Milliners** made hats especially for women. The name, milliner, comes from the name of a city in Italy. Milan was famous for producing women's fashions. Most hats were made to order. Customers described styles and the hatter made them.

# The wigmaker

Imagine waking up in the morning, getting dressed, and then being "wigged." In the eighteenth century, wearing wigs was the style for wealthy people. Wigs were popular, but they were expensive.

The wigmaker was also called the wigger, the wigster, the wig dresser, and the peruker. Perukers made, sold, and dressed wigs and false hair pieces. They also cut and styled people's natural hair and trimmed and shaved men's beards. Sometimes the peruker also pulled teeth!

Wigs were made to order. Each customer had a unique wig made especially for him or her. Each customer's head was measured. The peruker used these measurements to make a **caul**. The caul was a net cap. It was placed on a wooden wig block.

## A hairy job

The hair of the wig was attached to the caul. The most expensive wigs were made of human hair. Wigmakers thought women's hair made better wigs than men's hair. They also believed that a country woman's hair was better than a city woman's. The less expensive wigs were made of horsehair, calf hair, cow hair, or even from cotton and wool. The hair was cleaned and combed. The root ends of the hair were held in a special **vise** or clamp and the free ends were rolled onto curlers made of clay. The roots of the hair were attached to silk threads. The silk threads were stitched to the caul. The peruker followed a pattern when stitching the wig. The pattern told the peruker how many rows of hair were needed, how long each row must be, and how long the hair in each row must be. When the stitching was done, fringes of curled hair hung in layers.

## Ribbons and bows

The final step was to finish and dress the wig. The hair was shaped just right with fingers, combs, curling irons, and scissors. Ribbons, powder, and perfume were added if the customer wished. The wig was powdered with a brown, black, gray, or white color, depending on the latest fashion.

*The peruker puts on the finishing touch.*

*A wig plus a hat can get hot! This settler gives his head a breather as he reads his mail. His wife thinks he should put his wig back on.*

# Weaving chairs

In the early days, **rush** and **cane** chairs were fashionable. Rush seats were made with swamp rushes. They were woven tightly to form a thick seat. Cane seats were more delicate and less sturdy than rush seats. They were made with rattan or bamboo, which were imported from tropical countries. Rattan comes from the flexible stems of palm trees. Bamboo is a tall grass that looks like a tree. Cane chairs were usually put in the dining room, and rush seats were used in the kitchen.

Chair weavers often traveled from community to community. Sometimes a weaver was hired by a cabinetmaker. He then settled down to live in a village.

*Flat strips, called "standards," are being woven with wider strips, called "splints." Both kinds of strips were made of wood pounded flat.*

*This Indian woman earns her living by making and selling baskets. Baskets were necessary to the settlers. There were no shopping bags!*

# Making baskets

The early settlers knew it was not wise "to put all their eggs in one basket," but often that was the only practical way to carry them! There were no cardboard boxes or plastic bags in those days. People used light-weight baskets made of thin pieces of wood.

Basketry required patience and practice. Wooden baskets were made from oak, ash, or willow trees. Willow baskets were especially popular because they were light, yet strong. The wood was cut into long strips called **splints**. The splints were soaked in water to make them flexible.

When the splints were softened, they were pounded and flattened with a heavy hammer or mallet. Wood grows in layers. As the splints were pounded, the layers of wood started to split away from one another. The layers were carefully separated with a jack-knife. These strips were pounded again until they were very thin and flexible.

## Over and under

The weaver made the bottom of the basket first. The checker style of weave was common. The strips were woven under and over one another in a continuous pattern. After the bottom of the basket was formed, the strips were turned up to start the sides of the basket. The side strips were woven with other strips, called **standards**, which were placed around the basket. When the basket was tall enough, the tops of the strips were sharpened to points. The points were bent to fit into the last row of weaving. One strip was fitted around the top to form the rim, and another strip was used to make a handle.

*Pamela inspects a plate which has been glazed and fired. There was such a demand for her pottery that Pamela had to build a small factory behind her house. With the help of employees, Pamela is now able to supply several shops with her durable stoneware.*

# Pamela makes pottery

Pamela owns the village "pot house." She is the village potter. A few of the villagers buy delicate china imported from England, but most of them prefer Pamela's strong, brightly colored pots, plates, and cups.

Pamela collects the clay that she uses. She knows all the best places in which to find potter's clay. Only certain kinds of clay are suitable for making pots. She looks for clay with a reddish-brown color. After finding her supply, Pamela trudges home carrying her full pails. The raw clay is full of pebbles and plants. Pamela's first job is to clean out the dirt. She plunges the clay into a pail of water. Roots and leaves rise to the surface. Stones and pebbles fall to the bottom.

A potter's wheel stands in the corner of Pamela's pot house. The wheel is a round plate on a post. When Pamela pumps the foot pedal, the post and the plate spin.

## Shaping the clay

Pamela separates a bit of clay from the pile. She shapes it into a ball, and throws it on the wheel. She throws the clay hard, and she aims accurately. The clay lands smack on the middle of the wheel.

Pamela cups her hands around the clay and spins the wheel. This takes coordination! The spinning forces the clay against Pamela's hands. She makes a hollow in the ball by pressing her thumbs into the middle of the clay, while still cupping it between her palms. She now has a bowl.

Pamela carefully lifts the bowl off the wheel. The bowl must be bone-dry before it can be **fired** in the **kiln.** The kiln is an oven made of bricks. The clay bowl is put into the kiln. The fire bakes the clay for a day and a night. Then Pamela lets the fire die slowly. If the bowl is cooled quickly, it will split and crack.

*Glass was shaped by blowing it into a bubble and then swinging or twirling the bubble while it was still hot. Glass could also be rolled against a bar. It could be shaped with various tools. If the glass cooled while it was being shaped, it could be reheated and shaped again.*

## The finishing touch

The natural clays that Pamela uses must be **glazed** so that they will not leak. A glaze is a thin coating that looks like glass. Pamela makes glazes from lead and copper. One of the village boys grinds the metals into a fine powder. Pamela mixes a thick glaze and paints her pottery with it. The pottery is put back into the kiln. The heat turns the glaze into a coating which seals and protects the clay.

## Stoneware

Sometimes Pamela uses a special clay to make **stoneware**. Stoneware holds water and does not need a glaze. Clay for stoneware contains a large amount of **silica**, a hard chemical found in sand and quartz. When the kiln is at its hottest, Pamela opens the door and throws in some salt. The salt and silica combine to make the pottery hard.

## Glass blowers

There were no glass blowers among the early settlers. The settlers imported glass from Europe. The first glass blowers to work in this country were paid high wages because their skill was so valuable.

Glass was made with a mixture of sand and chemicals such as lime and soda. The mixture was heated in an extremely hot furnace so that it became a liquid. This liquid could be dropped into a mold and turned into a glass object. The liquid could also be blown into a shape. A glass blower blew into a pipe and created a bubble of glass. Then the bubble was shaped with tools. Glass windows were also made by glass blowers. A bubble of glass was blown and then spun into a sheet.

Glass articles had to be cooled slowly or else they would explode. They were placed in a hot oven which gradually cooled. Handles, spouts, and other small pieces were shaped separately. They were attached to teapots or cups by hot glass, which acted as a glue.

*The side panels of barrels and buckets were called "staves." Staves were shaped so that they formed a tight seal when put together.*

*The staves are together. The bottom and hoops are in place. This tub will be used for storing meat preserved in brine.*

# Barreling away

Have you ever imagined that you were a stowaway on a sailing ship? Where would you hide so that no one discovered that you were aboard? It would have to be a place where the crew would not look. It would have to be warm and dry, and large enough for you to fit comfortably. Perhaps your hiding place would be one of the large wooden barrels in the ship's hold.

The barrels, where provisions were stored for ocean voyages, had to be large and strong. Most barrels were big wooden containers which bulged in the middle. The wooden side panels were called **staves**. A stave was wider in the middle than at the ends. Staves were bound together at the top and bottom with metal hoops. The wide parts of the staves formed the barrel's bulge.

## The cooper's workshop

The artisans who made barrels were called **coopers**. There was a great demand for their products. They made barrels for all kinds of food. Flour barrels, pork barrels, meat and fish barrels, cider barrels, tubs, sap buckets, milk pails, and kitchen pails were all created by the cooper. Coopers were very important to the settler community. There were no cans or fancy packages for storing food.

There were three main steps in making a barrel. First, a **jointer** was used to cut wooden boards into staves. The jointer was a machine with a special blade. In the early days, many people earned their living by cutting these barrel staves.

*People carried water from the spring or well in buckets attached to a yoke. The yoke rested on the shoulders. The cooper made this equipment.*

*Coopers made piggins. Piggins were wooden pails with one stave left longer than the others. This stave served as the handle of the piggin.*

# Hooping the barrel

After the staves were cut and sanded, they were set inside a hoop made of wood or brass. Hoops were made by the **hooper**. They were adjustable. Matching pegs and holes fastened the hoop at the proper size. When the staves were bound at one end by the hoop, the other ends flared outward. At this stage, the barrel looked more like a tulip in full bloom than a watertight container!

Next came the tricky part. Getting the flared ends of the staves to come together was not easy! A special crank called a **windlass** was used. The windlass had a rope that went around the staves to gather the tops together. As the crank was turned, the tops were pulled tighter, until another hoop could be fitted around the staves. With the hoop in place, the rope was removed. A mallet was used to hammer the hoop even farther down around the belly of the barrel. A few smaller hoops were hammered on at both ends of the barrel

so that the staves were so tight that the barrel could hold water.

# From top to bottom

Finally, the **heads** were made. Heads were the top and bottom of a barrel. The cooper had to use a compass to draw the large circles. With a compass, the cooper was able to get a properly sized lid. When the wooden lids were cut, the cooper cut grooves on the ends of the staves so that the heads fit perfectly. If the barrel was to be used for storing liquid, the cooper would cut a little **bunghole** into one of the heads. This was used as a spout and was closed with a cork or wooden plug. Sometimes **spyholes** were cut into one side of the barrel so that people could check what was inside.

The farrier was a blacksmith who shod horses. Farriers were often **veterinarians,** too. They inspected the hoofs and legs of horses for injuries. The farrier, on the left, heats up the fire, while his apprentice shoes a horse. This picture shows how busy the settlers kept the blacksmith or farrier.

The blacksmith pulls the cord. The pull causes the bellows to contract and blow air on the fire in the forge to keep it hot.

The blacksmith takes the old shoes off with pincers. He cleans and trims the hoof before he nails the new shoe on.

# The village smithy

The blacksmith is familiar to most people, but how many of us know that "smith" comes from the verb meaning "to smite" or to hit? Did you know that "black" refers to the black metal the blacksmith used? The silversmith worked with bright metal. The blacksmith worked with iron.

When we think of the blacksmith, we first think of him in his role as **farrier**. We imagine him making a set of shoes for a horse. We picture him bent over his **anvil**. The anvil was the blacksmith's most important tool. It had a flat top on which hot iron could be hammered into shape. One end of the anvil was shaped like a pointed cone. It was used to make curved shapes. The blacksmith heated iron in his **forge**. The iron was shaped into a horseshoe. The blacksmith punched holes in the shoe.

## Shoeing horses

The blacksmith took the old shoes off the horse's hoofs with large **pincers**. He rested the hoofs against his leather apron as he cleaned them. Then he placed the new shoe on a hoof. He bent the iron until it fit perfectly. He nailed the shoe onto the hoof. The nails went through the holes he had made in the shoe. The nails did not hurt the horse. They went into the hard part of the hoof. Horses' hoofs are similar to our fingernails, which we cut and file without feeling any pain.

## Forging iron

In the early communities, the blacksmith also made iron tools for his neighbors. Iron forged on an anvil was called **wrought iron**. The blacksmith made wrought-iron tools for other craftspeople. He made iron tires for the wheelwright. The blacksmith made hinges , hooks, and latches for the cabinet-maker's fine furniture. He made weapons, cooking utensils, cutlery, and padlocks. Later, more and more iron tools and decorations were made in factories. The black-smith's main job became horseshoeing.

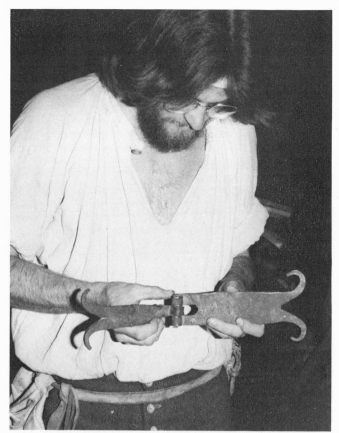

*Early blacksmiths also made weapons, cooking utensils, tools, nails, and padlocks. The black-smith in the picture shows a butterfly hinge.*

*Most of the early artisans were men. Women usually managed the home. These women work in the blacksmith shop to support their families.*

*Guns were a necessary part of early settler life. The settlers had to hunt for their food. They needed to protect themselves against wild animals. These settlers went hunting for deer. They needed meat for food and hide for clothing. This deer was shot, but is fighting back. Hunting could be dangerous.*

*These old guns have bayonets on their ends. Bayonets are sharp knives. These old guns make a beautiful wall decoration.*

# The gunsmith

A gun had three main parts. A person using a gun held onto the **stock** of the gun. The gunsmith whittled the stock out of walnut, maple, or persimmon wood. Sometimes the stock was made of metal. The **barrel** and the **flintlock** were attached to the stock. The barrel was a tube of iron, in which the ammunition for the gun was placed. The flintlock was a small mechanism that made the gun fire when its trigger was pulled.

The earliest guns were called **muzzle loaders.** They were given this name because gunpowder was poured into the muzzle, or the forward end of the gun barrel. The gunpowder was packed down to the end of the barrel with a **packing rod.** Then a **wad,** which was usually a piece of felt, was pushed down on top of the powder. A lead ball was packed on top of the wad.

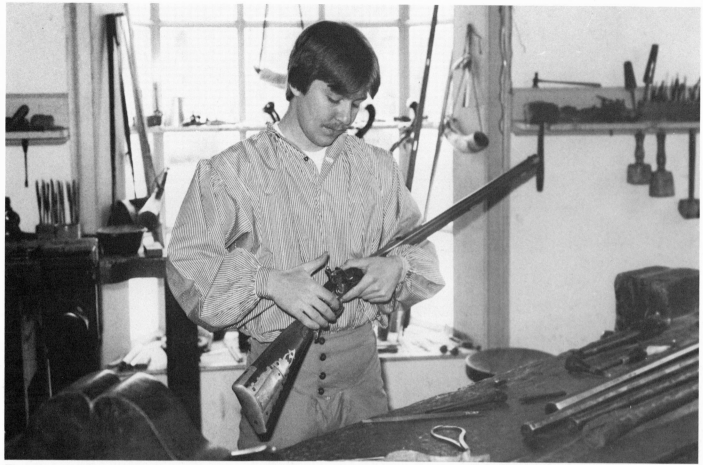

*The gunsmith's apprentice is holding a finished gun. The stock of the gun is decorated with brass. Gunsmiths were artists as well as metalworkers and woodworkers. The barrel is the end that is pointing to the right. The flintlock is located between the stock and the barrel.*

# Handle with care

Flint was used in the early guns to make the gunpowder explode. Flint makes a spark when it is struck by steel. The flint was in the flintlock. The flintlock included the flint, the **hammer**, and a **frizzen**. A frizzen was a little piece of steel that separated gunpowder from the hammer. When the trigger of the gun was pulled, the frizzen hit the flint and created sparks. The sparks lit a bit of the gunpowder and then all of the gunpowder exploded. The explosion of the gunpowder sent the lead ball shooting out of the barrel of the gun and toward the target.

Today, most people do not need to own guns. Some people still hunt, but usually hunting is a hobby. Each year many people are killed by guns. Guns are accurate and powerful weapons. They are dangerous in the hands of people who do not know how to use them. They are also dangerous in the hands of people who use guns for the wrong reasons.

*Mr. Graham sells guns that were made in factories. The parts can be replaced easily.*

Carriage-makers were called **wainwrights**. Wainwrights made the top part of carriages, wagons, and coaches. The wheels were made by the wheelwright. Wainwrights used white oak, white ash, and white elm for making the bodies of the carriages. They upholstered the seats in leather or cloth.

Wainwrights made cutters and sleighs. Often the upper part of the sleigh was made in the same way as the top part of the wagon. The difference between sleighs and carriages was that sleighs glided on blades while carriages rolled on wheels! Sleighs made winter travel easy and enjoyable.

# Wagons, carriages, and sleighs

The large carriage shop employed a variety of workers. Wheelwrights, blacksmiths, woodworkers, trimmers, upholsterers, and painters were all kept busy turning out beautiful carriages and wagons. The coaches were made with great care. Look at the shiny leather covering the seats.

Wainwrights never had a lazy day. Even when there were no orders for new wagons, old wagons were brought in to be repaired.

This old stagecoach ran in winter and summer. In the summer, the runners were replaced by wheels. Now that's a true convertible!

# Wheels!

How many machines, gadgets, and vehicles can you name that have wheels? The early settlers needed many sizes of wheels for their buggies, wagons, carts, wheelbarrows, and spinning wheels. The wheelwright made and repaired all the wheels the settlers needed.

*The wheelwright had names for the many parts of the wheel. In the center of the wheel was the **hub** or **nave.** The hub was the solid, circular piece in the middle of the wheel. It was often made from a section of a tree trunk. The wood for the hub was aged as long as seven years so that it would be perfectly dry. The hub was shaped on a lathe. This lathe was operated by turning the wheel by hand.*

*Holes, or **mortises,** were cut into the shaped hub. The mortises had to be perfectly positioned so that the wheel was well balanced. The **spokes** were driven into the holes with a heavy mallet.*

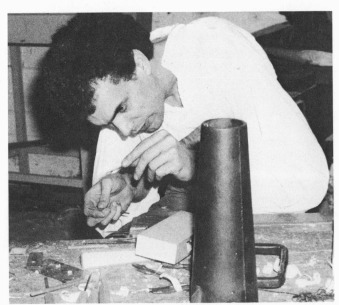

*A hollow cone of bronze or iron was placed inside the hub of the wheel. This cone was called a **box.** It was made by the blacksmith.*

The hub held the spokes in place. Spokes were the long wooden rods that radiated from the hub. The hub and spokes together were called a **spider.** Does this look like a spider to you?

The other ends of the wooden spokes fit into the **fellies.** Fellies were curved pieces of wood. The spokes were tapered so they could fit into the holes in the fellies.

Large wheels were strengthened by a metal ring called a **tire.** The blacksmith, or some-times the wheelwright himself, shaped the ring after heating it in a forge. By the time the ring was bent to the right size, it was red-hot. After it was placed around the rim of the wheel, a cold bucket of water was thrown on the hot metal. The cold water made the ring shrink. It tightened around the wheel, locking the parts together.

After the fellies were matched with the spokes, the spokes were hammered into the fellies. The fellies were lined up to make the rim of the wheel.

*Harnessmakers used leather to make saddles, pouches, saddlebags, and other harness.  The harness-maker was one of the busiest artisans in a settler community.  The **clam** was one of his most important tools.  It was like a third hand.  It held a piece of leather in place and left the artisan's hands free.*

*Horses and oxen provided power for land transportation. Wagons and carriages were hitched to these animals by harnesses. Reins steered the animals. Blinders made horses keep their eyes on the road! This old stable shows leather objects made by the harnessmaker. Can you find them?*

# The harnessmaker

What would the early farmer have done without his horses or his oxen? These animals pulled the plow and harrow. They helped the farmer plant and harvest food. They also pulled the farmer on journeys along the rough roads. The horses and oxen were attached to carts and wagons by harness. The harness made it possible for the farmer to use the great pulling strength of these animals.

Wherever there were horses or oxen, there were harnessmakers. They made the reins, the traces, the breeching, the bellybands, the crupper, the headstall, and all the other pieces that formed the complicated harness. The harness was made of leather. The best leather was used for the pieces of the harness that bore the most stress, such as the girth strap. If the girth strap was of poor quality, it would stretch. Leather of a poorer quality was used to make pieces that did not have to bear stress, such as **blinkers**. Blinkers were placed at each side of a horse's head so that the animal could not be distracted by seeing what was beside it. The farmer did not have to order a special harness to fit each animal. The harnessmaker had an "elastic model." This was a harness with straps that could be lengthened to fit a big ox, or be taken in to fit a small horse.

## Cutting and stitching

The harnessmaker spread the leather on a broad table. He cut the hide to the proper sizes and shapes. Then he put each piece of leather between the **clam**. The clam was a wooden clamp with jaws. It looked like the shell of a clam. The clam held the leather, leaving both hands free.

The leather was marked by a pricking wheel, to show where the seams would be sewn. This wheel was a roller with sharp points that made evenly spaced dots on the leather. The harnessmaker pierced holes with an awl where these marks appeared. The leather was then stitched with a needle and cord.

## Decorating the leather

The harnessmaker was an artist who took pride in his work. He liked to make handsome saddles, adding designs to the leather. Some harnesses were decorated with bits of brass in different shapes. These decorations were called **amulets**.

*A house will soon be built on this spot. Workers have been busy making bricks for it. You can see the pugmill. It mixes clay with water. The mixed clay comes out the bottom. The frame that molds the clay into bricks leans against the pugmill.*

*Children carry clay which will be used to make bricks. The machine lifts clay from a swampy clay pit. Children often worked at hard jobs.*

# Brickworks

The first settler homes were built of logs. Later, brick homes became common. Brick builders were important members of the growing communities.

Brick builders gathered clay from river banks and transported it to the site where the house was to be constructed. The clay was mixed with water in a **pugmill**. A pugmill was made up of a wooden post and a cylinder. The cylinder, which held water, encircled the lower half of the post. This part of the post had pegs on it, arranged in a downward spiral. The whole post was rotated by water, steam, or animal power. As the post rotated, the pegs mixed the clay and water into a stiff paste. The spiral arrangement of the pegs pushed the clay downward. There was a slot in the bottom of the cylinder. The laborers took the stiff clay from this slot, as they needed it.

*Workers are building a house. Many of the first homes in this town were built of wood. Later, brick homes also became practical and popular. Large cut stones form the foundation. Small bricks are stacked to make walls. The construction industry grew as more people moved to this country.*

## Molding and firing

The clay was put into a brick mold. The brick mold was easy to make. It was a box divided with boards. The box contained six or eight spaces. Each space was the size of a brick.

The mold was put in water and then dipped in sand. The sand prevented the bricks from sticking in the mold. Clay was pressed into each partition. A board was used to scrape the excess clay from the top of the mold. After the bricks were shaped, they were dumped out of the molds onto a rack. They were left to dry for two weeks.

The bricks were put into a **kiln** to be hardened. The kiln was made of several walls of bricks and had tunnels and openings so that heat from a fire could circulate. The fire burned 24 hours a day for 10 days. When the bricks were cooled, they were as hard as rocks.

*Plastering perfectly took practice! Quickly and neatly, workers made walls and ceilings smooth. Plaster was made of lime, sand, and water.*

41

The itinerant tinker was a busy worker. He traveled from village to village fixing pots and pans made from tin. Tin was imported from Europe in big sheets. The tinsmith hammered this tin into useful objects, such as spoons, cups, and plates. The tinsmith was also known as the whitesmith. A blacksmith worked with iron, which is black. The tinsmith worked with tin, which is light in color. The pots made by the tinsmith were popular when stoves replaced fireplaces. They were much lighter than the iron pots needed to cook over fire. However, tin pots wore out much faster. When tin pots and pans wore out, the tinker fixed them. The tinsmith created the job of the tinker.

*Candlesticks were made from gold, silver, brass, pewter, and tin. The settlers had no electricity. Each family owned several kinds of candlesticks.*

*The cutler used steel to make knives, scissors, sickles, saws, and other cutting instruments. This cutler is sharpening dull instruments.*

# Metalworkers

Metal was rare in the New World. There were few mines to gather the different metals from under the ground. Most metal was imported from Europe. Often people sold their metal possessions to metalworkers, who melted the objects down and made new utensils.

Metalworkers made buckles, buttons, candlesticks, dishes, spoons, and cups. They used copper, pewter, tin, silver, and brass. Copper **warming pans** were popular. The pan held hot coals. It was put between bed sheets to warm them up. Pewter was molded into spoons and plates. The tinsmith made weather vanes, lanterns, and pots. The silversmith made beautiful tableware. Brass was used to form bells, tools for surgery, and parts for guns and clocks.

Some metals, such as pewter, were molded. Often the pieces of a product were **cast** or set in a mold. Then the pieces were **soldered** or joined together. Some metals were hammered into sheets. The sheets were cut and shaped before being soldered together.

*Copper has a bright, reddish-brown color. The coppersmith made kettles and other beautiful and useful objects with this metal.*

Some metalworkers made special parts for other artisans, such as the gunsmith and clockmaker. This metalworker specialized in gears and other small machine parts. He made these parts to order. In later days, as factories produced many goods, parts were **standardized**. Thousands of parts were made following one standard pattern. These parts could be replaced easily when they wore out.

44

The silversmith was often the jeweler as well. The artisan polishes rings and bracelets. He made the jewelry by pounding thin strips of silver and then **soldering** them. After the rings and bracelets are polished, they will be ready to sell. The jeweler will display them in a glass cabinet.

There were few banks where money could be stored. Settlers often gave silver coins to the silversmith to be melted down. The silversmith made bowls, cups, and other objects from the silver. An engraver put the settlers' initials into the objects so that they would not be stolen.

The pewterer uses a lathe to put designs on a cup. Pewter is made of tin and a bit of lead or copper. This **alloy** was poured into molds and then cooled.

45

Amanda has woken again! Her father, the town cabinetmaker, made the wooden part of this beautiful grandfather clock. The clockmaker worked for days hammering the delicate brass design inside the glass door. Making gears to turn at just the right speed took weeks. Finally, the work of art was brought home, but no one told Amanda about the noise — DONG! DONG! DONG! — all night long!

*The clockmaker made only the inside of the clock. Jed watches his grandfather, the clockmaker, repair a gear in a clock he made.*

*The first watches in this country were imported. Watchmakers worked at repairing these watches. People wore their watches on chains.*

# Time for clocks

The weather was the most important calendar for the early settlers. They worked according to the season. The height of the sun and the length of the shadows told the time of day. The early settlers did not need a watch or a clock to tell them when to rise or to go to bed. As settlements were established, merchants, bankers, storekeepers, and doctors set up their businesses. These people had appointments to keep. Hourglasses and sundials were used, but even more accurate methods of telling time were needed.

## Pendulums and gears

The early clockmaker was responsible only for making the inner part of a clock. The cabinetmaker built the case for the gears. The case protected the gears from dust and made the clock a beautiful decoration. The **pendulum** and the weights of the pendulum were attached to the gears. Most early clocks were made of brass. The brass was cast in a mold. The clockmaker worked for days, hammering the brass until it was stiff and thin. The gears were cut out of this brass with a file. Some of the early clockmakers also made wooden clocks. Unfortunately, the wooden cogs in the gears often split. In damp weather, the gears sometimes swelled and stopped. Some wooden clocks were kept in a dry place and lasted for more than one hundred years.

## Grandfather clocks

Most early clockmakers made tall clocks or "grandfather clocks." These clocks had only an hour hand. They were very expensive. In later days, clockmakers were able to make smaller clocks, which were attached to the wall or placed on a shelf.

# Printing from A to Z

Early settlers looked forward to receiving the newspaper. Although many people could not read, newspapers were the best way to learn the news. People gathered around the best reader in the family to hear the news. When important laws were passed, the newspaper reported them. Newspapers informed people of the promises that election candidates made. Readers wrote letters stating their opinions. The paper published these "letters to the editor." The newspaper was also entertaining. It contained many poems, stories, riddles, and puzzles.

## Almanacs

Almanacs were another good source of information. Almanacs gave the weather forecasts for an entire year! Farmers consulted almanacs before they planted their crops. Sailors used almanacs to find out about ocean tides. People also enjoyed the short stories, comics, and recipes.

## Setting the type

Today, the news is printed quickly by huge machines. Early printers did not have sophisticated printing presses. What we can do with the touch of a button took several people many hours to accomplish. Today, news stories are typed into computers. Each letter and punctuation mark in the early newspaper was put in place one by one. The **compositor** worked at this painstaking task.

*The letters of type, or characters, were stored according to their sizes in the shallow drawers shown in the background of this picture. The compositor is setting the letters on the composition stick.*

*The columns formed on the composition stick have been put into the galley, which is now full. The compositor locks the type into the galley.*

*The galley looks beautiful! Notice that the type is backwards. When it is imprinted on paper, the copy will read normally. Printing was hard work!*

# The compositor's job

The compositor was given the **copy** or material that was to be printed. She chose the correct letters, or **characters**, from shallow trays that were called **type cases**. The characters were stuck on tiny pieces of metal or wood. The type cases had little compartments. Each compartment contained many copies of one letter of the alphabet. After several years of practice, a good compositor could choose characters without looking at the type case!

The compositor placed the selected letters on a **composition stick**. The characters on this stick were put in even rows of words.

The rows of words on the composition stick formed columns. The characters were placed upside down and backwards. When they were imprinted on a page, the words appeared in the correct position. Spacers were needed to separate words. The compositor was also responsible for punctuation.

The most difficult part of the job was **justifying** the edges of the columns, or **margins**. The compositor had to add or subtract spacers so that the right-hand margin was as straight as the left. This made the columns neat and easy to read when they were printed. This paragraph has been justified. Can you see the extra spaces between words?

After the composition stick was full, the compositor placed it on a large tray called a **galley**. A galley was the same size as a newspaper page. The compositor made a **proof** of the galley after it was filled with columns. She spread ink over the type and then pressed a piece of newsprint down on top of it. When the paper was pulled off, a rough copy of the newspaper page was ready for proofreading. A copy editor searched for errors and marked them so that the compositor would find them easily. Each mistake was carefully corrected.

*The ink must be spread evenly so that it will not make blots on the printed sheet. The ink roller is pushed over a hard surface covered with ink. When the roller was coated evenly, it was rolled over the galley. Then the inked galley was ready to be put into the press.*

*"Ink balls" were used instead of rollers by early printers. This older method of inking with a leather pad often did not leave an even coat.*

## The stoneman's job

The corrected galleys were sent to the **stone-man.** The stoneman put the galleys together to make **forms.** The pages that would be printed on the same form were chosen according to the way in which the pages would be folded. (Folding is described in the following section on bookbinding.) A space was always left between galleys, where the pages would be folded. When the forms were finished, the pages were ready for the printing press.

*Blank paper was attached to the press (left side). Paper was scarce because there were no paper mills. In the early days, some paper was made from linen rags. The rags were mixed with water until the fibers in the fabric separated. This **pulp** of fibers was pressed into sheets. Some people still call newspapers "rags" because the paper was made from fabric. The blank paper on the press was closed over the inked type. The two panels were slid under the press. The press squeezed the paper against the inked type. The panels you see have been pulled out of the press. You can see the new imprinted pages.*

# Fit to print

It is easy to figure out why these machines were called "presses." Printing presses were worked by hand. A thick, black or indigo ink was spread evenly over the type. A sheet of paper was placed on a wooden frame. A handle was pulled to press the inked type against the paper. This sheet was removed from the press. Then the other side of the sheet was printed. If the printed sheet had more than one page on each side, the sheet would be folded. Then the pages were put in the correct order. The newspaper or almanac was ready to read.

The bookbinder stitches the signatures together at the sewing frame. He uses strong thread made from linen. He loops the thread through the folds of the signatures and binds them to the cords attached to the sewing frame.

After the stitching is finished, the binder glues the spine. Next, the cover boards will be put on. Old books have ridges on their spines because the cords make bumps in the leather.

# Binding books

My father is a bookbinder. I love to sit quietly in his shop while he works slowly at his craft. I like to hold the books when they are bound. They have the wonderful, dark smell of leather. When you run your fingers over the covers, you can feel the ridges and hollows of the designs that my father has stamped into the leather. I think that my father is a true artist.

Many people buy the printed sheets of a book and bring them to my father to bind. People admire the rich, dark colors of red, blue, green, brown, and black that my father chooses for the covers. Some customers want a special shade of leather and a special design made with hot brass tools. They have all the books in their libraries bound to match.

When my father receives the insides of a book, I help him to fold the printed pages. I must not fold the pages in the wrong order! Folding pages, believe it or not, is difficult! Sometimes we fold each printed sheet once, to make a tall book. One fold makes four pages. Try it yourself! Take a blank piece of paper. On one side, draw the diagram on the left. Pick up the right corner of your diagram and turn the paper over. Draw the right diagram. Fold your paper in the middle. Can you read "This is a folio"?

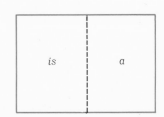

A **quarto** is eight pages. You must cut the two top folds. Fold these pages and read "Quartos are more difficult. You fold them twice."

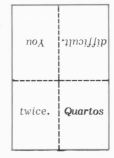
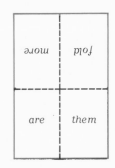

**Octavos** are the most difficult. They must be folded three times. When you cut the folds, the octavo will have sixteen pages.

*Colored endpapers were made by dropping different dyes into a heavy syrup. The colors did not blend or mix. A type of comb was used to "marble" the colors, creating interesting designs. The endpapers were carefully placed into the dyes. Marbling was a popular method for coloring endpapers.*

## Stitching the signatures

Each folded sheet, no matter how many times it is folded, is called a **signature**. The signatures are put into the correct page order. Then Father stitches the signatures to little cords. Many of the edges of the pages are still folded. You cannot turn the pages of the book! The pages must be trimmed. Sometimes people cut the folds as they read through the book for the first time.

## Pasting the endpapers

The next step is to cut **pasteboard** for the covers of the book. Pasteboard is made with pieces of paper that have been glued together and rolled into flat, hard boards. Pasteboards form the covers of the books. They are attached to the cords that hold the pages together. Then the pasteboards are covered with cloth, paper, or leather. Some bookbinders cover the board with sheepskin. My father will not use anything but leather. Books deserve the best leather, he says.

When you open a book, you often see that the insides of the front and back covers have pieces of paper pasted onto them. Father often uses a pretty blue for these **endpapers**. Sometimes he uses a special paper decorated with gold pictures. Then the book is tied up tightly so that it will dry with everything in its proper position.

When the glue is dry, the title of the book is stamped on a strip of leather. After the strip is decorated, it is glued onto the **spine** of the book. The book is ready to be read.

# The growth of business

*In the early days, the work of the artisans was called the "cottage industry." The artisans worked in their homes, or cottages. As factories were built, more products were made in the towns and cities. Peddlers, such as this one, were like traveling salesmen. They sold the products made in factories.*

The family is eager to see the products that this peddler carries in his wagon. He brings fine fabrics, shiny pots, strong pails, and stiff brooms which were made in factories. Before long, people opened stores in towns and filled the shelves with these products. Factory-made products became common.

Small factories, such as this one, provided work for many people who did not work in their own small businesses. These men are blind. They are making brooms from "broomcorn," a special grass with strong stalks. Many businesses opened as villages and towns grew.

# Arts and crafts

*The settlers loved masquerades. They held masquerade parties around Christmas time, in the spring, or for just about any occasion. Sometimes the settlers dressed in costumes when they went skating. There were also "fancy dress" parties in the cities. Masks were an important part of costumes.*

If the early settlers wanted a picture of themselves, they had two choices. They could have a picture painted, or they could have a silhouette maker cut out their profile in black paper. In the 1850s, traveling photographers started to appear. Settlers flocked to have their pictures taken.

Taxidermists preserved the bodies of dead animals. They stuffed animals killed by hunters. They put exotic animals on display.

As the settlers found they had more free time, they turned to arts such as painting. This man is painting the beautiful country landscape.

*Shipyards were started where there was a port and people skilled in the craft of building ships. The captains of foreign ships often hired out their sailors to help in the shipyards. Often these skilled sailors stayed in the New World to become shipbuilders.*

# Setting sail!

The settlers had no telephones or radios. Flying in airplanes was just a dream. The only way to communicate with people or travel across the sea was by ship. The settlers also used ships and boats when they harvested fish from the sea. Shipbuilders were dedicated artisans. Building a ship was a huge job.

Ships were built at the water's edge. Trees were cut from the thick forests. Each shipyard had its own sawmill for making lumber from the trees. The shipbuilder designed a model of the **hull** or frame of the ship. He worked from this model to make sure that the ship was built properly. The frame of the ship

*Ships needed sails. This group of men found jobs at the shipyard. They became sailmakers. Sails had to be cut and stitched by hand. It took these men many days to complete the sails needed for a big ship. Today, the same sails could be made by machines in minutes.*

was built first. The frame was braced by the strongest pieces of timber. It was covered, inside and outside, with planks of wood.

The seams between the planks were sealed carefully to prevent water from leaking into the ship. The seams were first stuffed with **oakum.** Rope was untwisted and pulled apart. The hemp fibers of rope were called oakum. After the seams were stuffed, they were covered with hot **pitch.** Pitch is a thick, dark, sticky substance made from tar. The bottom of the ship was tarred and then covered with copper. After all of this waterproofing, wooden ships still leaked. Sailors had to pump the **bilge** every day. The bilge is the rounded part at the bottom of a ship.

# Wanted: artisans of all kinds!

Shipbuilding attracted people with many skills. Blacksmiths, painters, carpenters, netmakers, ropemakers, and sailmakers moved to towns and cities with ports. These people made the parts needed to clothe the bare wooden frame. Sails were stitched and

raised. Furniture was built for the sailors' quarters. Blacksmiths made the iron fittings needed on the ship. **Forgers** made the anchors, which no ship could do without.

The big event for shipbuilders was the launching ceremony. The ceremony took place when the ship was finished and still on dry land. The builders wished their ship luck and safety. Today, people often christen ships by giving them names. In the early days, the oldest sailor present had this honor. A clergyman also blessed the ship. Slowly the great ship slipped into the water. It embarked on its long career!

Before textile mills, the settlers had to card, spin, and weave their own wool. The machines in the textile factories made beautiful materials in different colors and with different patterns. The settlers could now buy fabrics at the general store, or from the tailor or dressmaker.

Hats and more hats! The settlers loved them. The women in this hat factory each add one part to the hat. Thousands of hats could be made quickly on this assembly line.

*This barrel factory can turn out many barrels in a day. Each worker has a different job to do. The machine can pull the staves of a barrel together easily. The early cooper used all his strength and a windlass to bend the staves. Some of these factory workers were once independent coopers.*

# Assembly lines

In the early days, the artisans were very important to the settler community. They made the useful — and beautiful — objects that the settlers needed. As factories opened in the towns and cities, more and more products could be bought ready-made. These products were cheaper because they could be made quickly by machines. Products made by hand took many hours to finish. The artisans were paid for all the time they spent making an object. Many artisans found that they could not compete with the factories. The settlers could buy **manufactured** goods at lower prices.

There were several reasons for the growth of factories. The artisans used fire, water, animals, and their own hands as sources of power. As new **sources of power**, such as steam and electricity, were discovered, bigger and better machines were built. These machines were able to produce objects faster than human beings could.

The invention of **standardized parts** meant that factory-made products were easier to manufacture. Standardized parts are machine parts that are exactly the same shape and size as one another. An old standardized part could be replaced easily when it wore out. Standardized parts and the introduction of the **assembly line** increased the speed at which products could be put together. On the assembly line a worker would stay in one place in a line of machines and other workers. One worker added a part to a product. The next worker added the next part, and so on, until the product was completed.

Products made with standardized parts, on assembly lines, and with new sources of power, cost less to make. Products could be sold for less money because they were not expensive to manufacture. The settlers could buy many things that they could not afford before.

Factories made life better, but there was also a sad side to the growth of industry. Many artisans found themselves without work. The settlers bought cheaper manufactured goods from large department stores in the towns and cities. They no longer ordered furniture or shoes from individual artisans. They purchased factory-made chairs and boots. The artisans were forced to look for employment in factories. Their special skills were no longer needed. The spirit of independence, which was an important part of the life of an artisan, was carried away by the assembly line.

# That special quality

Factories made products quickly and inexpensively. These products were advertised in newspapers and sold in big department stores. People were able to buy things they could never afford before. As products from factories appeared in smaller towns and villages, the settlers wanted to buy them instead of handmade products. The factory-made items were new and exciting to the settlers.

Today, people appreciate the quality of the products made by the early artisans. An object made by hand is just a little different from any other. It is unique. Objects made by hand in the past have become valuable antiques. People pay high prices to own these antiques. They were made with such skill and care that they are still strong and beautiful.

Many people today have taken the time to learn the skills of the early artisans. We can buy handmade products created with the same care and imagination as the products used by the settlers. Today, people appreciate handcrafted furniture, pottery, jewelry, and toys. Factories still make most of the goods that we enjoy. It is good to know, however, that the skills of the early artisans are still alive today. The quality of the objects made by artisans will never be old-fashioned.

# Glossary

**alloy** a metal made by mixing two or more metals

**almanac** a book published every year giving facts about many subjects

**antique** furniture, silver, and other things made long ago

**anvil** a heavy block of iron or steel with a flat top on which metals can be shaped

**apprentice** a person who works for a skilled worker in order to learn a trade

**artisan** a person trained and skilled in a craft

**auger** a tool for boring holes

**awl** a pointed tool for making small holes in wood or leather

**card** to untangle and straighten fibers of wool with an instrument or machine

**cast** to shape something by pouring it into a mold

**circulate** to spread or move about

**cog** a tooth on the edge of a wheel

**cutter** a small sleigh

**cylinder** a container in the shape of a tube

**decoy** a model of a duck or other bird used by hunters to attract real birds

**ebony** a hard and heavy tree that grows in tropical countries; its wood is used to make the black keys of pianos

**eighteenth century** the years 1701 to 1800

**gears** a wheel with teeth around the edge, which fit into the teeth of another wheel

**grain** the lines that form a pattern in wood

**harpsichord** an instrument similar to a piano

**harrow** a tool used to loosen and level soil

**import** to bring in products from another country

**indigo** a dark-blue dye

**lumberjack** a person whose work is to cut down trees and take them to the sawmill

**luster** the shine or glow of a surface

**mallet** a hammer with a wooden head

**pendulum** a weight hung by a cord or bar so that it can swing back and forth

**persimmon** a North American tree with a sweet and juicy orange-red fruit

**pincers** an instrument used for gripping

**prow** the forward part of a ship or boat

**radiate** to branch out from the center

**shellac** a liquid used to give a hard and shiny coat to furniture and floors; a kind of varnish

**shuttle** the part on a loom that carries yarn back and forth across the yarn that is already strung on the loom

**sickle** a tool with a sharp, curved blade and a short handle, used to cut grain

**silhouette** the outline of an object, usually filled in with black or a dark color

**site** the place where something is located

**soldering** joining metal with melted metal

**spine** the part of a book you see when the book is on a shelf — a book's "backbone"

**spinet** an instrument like a small harpsichord

**stringed instrument** a musical instrument, such as a violin, that has strings which produce notes when plucked or played with a bow

**taper** to make thinner at one end

**upholsterer** a person who works at covering furniture with cushions and material

**varnish** a liquid, used on furniture, that dries into a thin, hard surface

**weather vane** a flat piece of wood or metal, moved by the wind, which shows the direction the wind is blowing

**whittle** to make something by cutting away small pieces from wood with a knife

**yoke** a frame carried by animals or people which makes pulling or carrying a load easier

# Index

# Acknowledgements

Library of Congress, Dover Archives, Colonial Williamsburg, Century Village, Lang, Upper Canada Village, Black Creek Pioneer Village, Metropolitan Toronto Library, Colborne Lodge, Toronto Historical Board, Gibson House, City of Toronto Archives, Bibliotheque National du Quebec, Harper's Weekly, Canadian Illustrated News, Public Archives of Canada, Notman Photographic Archives, Little Wide Awake, Frank Leslie's Illustrated Magazine, the Osborne Collection of Early Children's Books, Toronto Public Library, the Buffalo and Erie County Public Library Rare Book Department, Jamestown, Chatterbox, McCord Museum, Harper's Round Table Magazine, Peterborough Postcard Company, John. P. Robarts Library.

12131415 LB Printed in the U.S.A. 98765